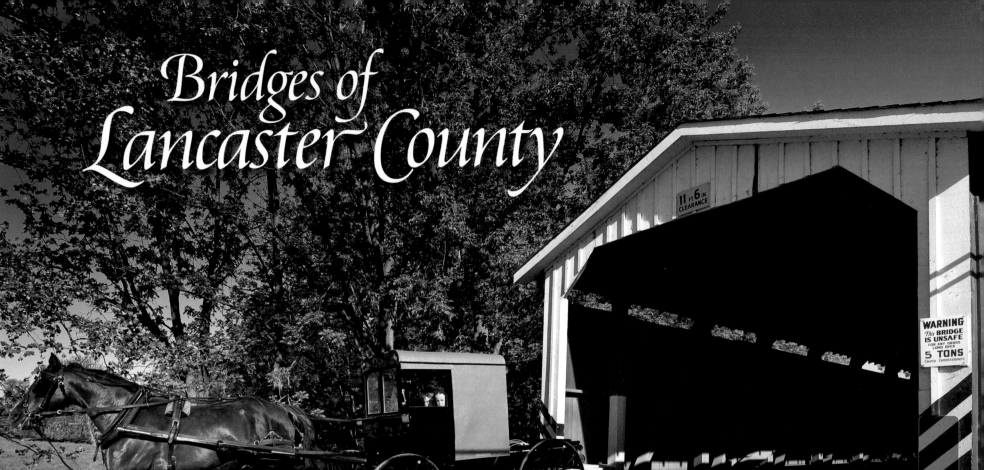

Bridges of
Lancaster County

Bruce M. Waters

Schiffer Publishing Ltd

4880 Lower Valley Road Atglen, Pennsylvania 19310

WARNING
This BRIDGE
IS UNSAFE
FOR ANY GROSS
LOAD OVER
5 TONS
County Commissioners

11 FT 6 IN.
CLEARANCE

Dedication

To my wife Susan with all my love.

Other Schiffer Books on Related Subjects
Lancaster County, Pennsylvania, Postcards: Featuring the Collection of the Landis Valley Museum. Irwin Richman. ISBN: 9780764329708. $29.99

Designed by Bruce M. Waters
Type set in Goudy Oldstyle

ISBN: 978-0-7643-3427-6
Printed in Hong Kong

Schiffer Books are available at special discounts for bulk purchases for sales promotions or premiums. Special editions, including personalized covers, corporate imprints, and excerpts can be created in large quantities for special needs. For more information contact the publisher:

Published by Schiffer Publishing Ltd.
4880 Lower Valley Road
Atglen, PA 19310
Phone: (610) 593-1777; Fax: (610) 593-2002
E-mail: Info@schifferbooks.com

For the largest selection of fine reference books on this and related subjects, please visit our web site at **www.schifferbooks.com**
We are always looking for people to write books on new and related subjects. If you have an idea for a book please contact us at the above address.

This book may be purchased from the publisher.
Include $5.00 for shipping.
Please try your bookstore first.
You may write for a free catalog.

In Europe, Schiffer books are distributed by
Bushwood Books
6 Marksbury Ave.
Kew Gardens
Surrey TW9 4JF England
Phone: 44 (0) 20 8392 8585; Fax: 44 (0) 20 8392 9876
E-mail: info@bushwoodbooks.co.uk
Website: www.bushwoodbooks.co.uk

Contents

Introduction 4

Lancaster City Loop Tour 7

Hunsecker's Mill Bridge 9

Pinetown Bridge 13

Landis Mill Bridge 17

Kurtz Mill Bridge 21

Willow Hill Bridge 25

Chickies Creek Tour 27

Shearer's Bridge 29

Shenck's Mill Bridge 31

Siegrist's Mill Bridge 35

Forry's Mill Bridge 39

Pequea Creek Tour 43

Leaman's Place Bridge 45

Herr's Mill Bridge 49

Neff's Mill Bridge 51

Lime Valley Bridge 55

Baumgardener's Mill Bridge 57

Colemanville Bridge 61

Octoraro Creek Loop Tour 65

Jackson's Mill Bridge 67

White Rock Bridge 71

Pine Grove Bridge 75

Mercer's Mill Bridge 81

Northeastern Lancaster County Loop Tour ... 85

Bucher's Mill Bridge 87

Erb's Bridge 91

Bitzer's Mill Bridge 95

Red Run Bridge 99

Weaver's Mill Bridge 103

Pool Forge Bridge 107

Introduction

In the early 1800s the state of Pennsylvania had over 1,500 covered bridges. Today that number has dwindled to just over 200, with Lancaster County containing the most bridges in the state.

Why does anyone cover a bridge in the first place? Considering that the bridges were constructed from wood, they were covered to provide protection from the destructive effects of weather, thus greatly extending the life of the bridge. Regrettably many covered bridges have been replaced with modern reinforced concrete and steel beam bridges.

In 1972, Hurricane Agnes took a great toll on many covered bridges in Lancaster County. Due to flooding, a number of bridges were either damaged or destroyed; some were rebuilt, while others were replaced by concrete spans.

The bridges of Lancaster County are all built employing similar construction methods, making use of the Burr arch truss. The architecture of the Burr arch was designed so that the arch would be capable of supporting the entire load of the bridge while the trusses would keep the bridge rigid and form a framework for the roof. The combination of the arch and truss provides a more stable platform capable of carrying greater weight than either the truss or the arch by itself.

Many of the bridges were built by the same man, Elias McMellen, who built twelve of the existing bridges. Most of the Lancaster County bridges are painted with red sides and white portals. This color scheme seems to have been exported from the European tradition of bridge painting.

To make this tour of the bridges of Lancaster County as convenient and safe as possible, the author has provided GPS Coordinates to locate each bridge using your cars satellite navigation system. The bridges have been grouped into five discrete tours as seen on the following map. By using the GPS Coordinates you can begin your tour from any location and change or edit the sequence as your mood or time allows.

So enjoy the twenty-five bridges presented here and be sure to buckle-up.

Top photo showing the arching Burr truss and king post side construction. Photo below showing the Burr truss anchored in the bridge's foundation.

Lancaster County, Pennsylvania

Northeastern Lancaster County Loop

Bucher's Mill Bridge

Erb's Bridge

Shearer's Bridge

Manheim

Lititz

Red Run Bridge

Shenck's Mill Bridge

Bitzer's Mill Bridge

Weaver's Mill Bridge

Siegrist's Mill Bridge

Ephrata

Mt. Joy

Pool Forge Bridge

Chickies Creek Tour

Pinetown Bridge

New Holland

Landis Mill Bridge

Hunsecker's Mill Bridge

Forry's Mill Bridge

Willow Hill Bridge

Lancaster

Leman's Place Bridge

Lancaster City Loop

Herr's Mill Bridge

Kurtz Mill Bridge

Susquehanna River

Neff's Mill Bridge

Strasburg

Pequea Creek Tour

Mercer's Mill Bridge

Lime Valley Bridge

Jackson's Mill Bridge

Baumgardener's Mill Bridge

Colemanville Bridge

Quarryville

Octoraro Creek Loop

White Rock Bridge

Pine Grove Bridge

Lancaster City Loop Tour

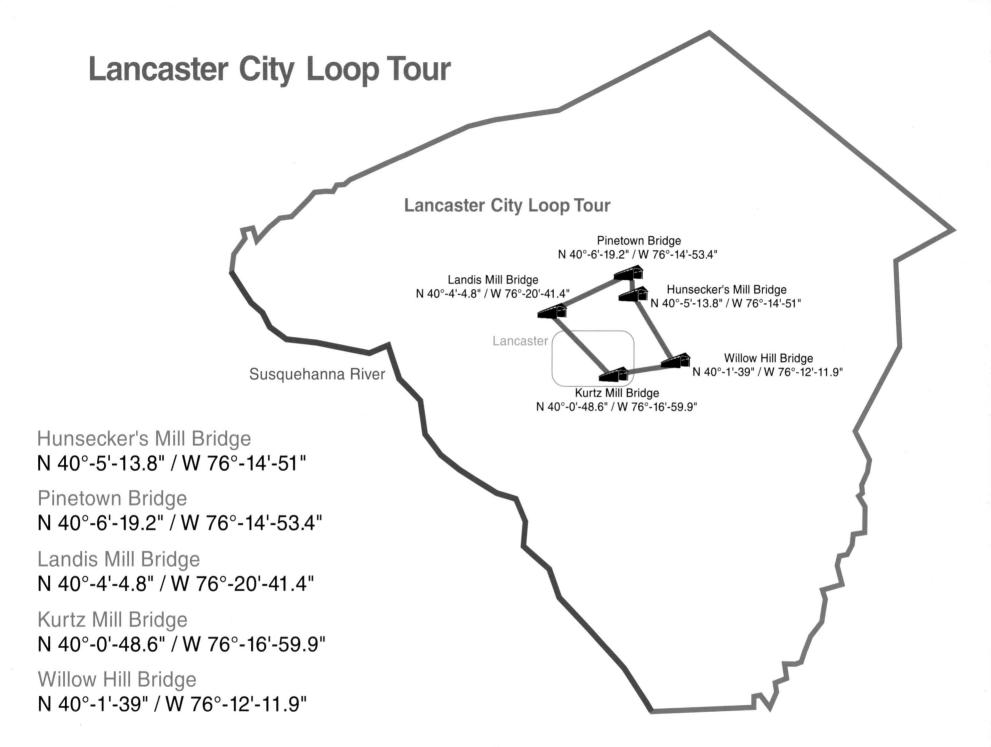

Lancaster City Loop Tour

Pinetown Bridge
N 40°-6'-19.2" / W 76°-14'-53.4"

Landis Mill Bridge
N 40°-4'-4.8" / W 76°-20'-41.4"

Hunsecker's Mill Bridge
N 40°-5'-13.8" / W 76°-14'-51"

Lancaster

Willow Hill Bridge
N 40°-1'-39" / W 76°-12'-11.9"

Susquehanna River

Kurtz Mill Bridge
N 40°-0'-48.6" / W 76°-16'-59.9"

Hunsecker's Mill Bridge
N 40°-5'-13.8" / W 76°-14'-51"

Pinetown Bridge
N 40°-6'-19.2" / W 76°-14'-53.4"

Landis Mill Bridge
N 40°-4'-4.8" / W 76°-20'-41.4"

Kurtz Mill Bridge
N 40°-0'-48.6" / W 76°-16'-59.9"

Willow Hill Bridge
N 40°-1'-39" / W 76°-12'-11.9"

7

Hunsecker's Mill Bridge

GPS Coordinates: N 40°-5'-13.8" / W 76°-14'-51"

History: Built in 1843 by John Russell at a cost of $1,988 the bridge was nearly destroyed by Hurricane Agnes in 1972, but was rebuilt the following year. Its length of 180 ft. makes it the longest single span covered bridge in the county.

Length: 180 feet
Width: 15 feet

River Crossed: Conestoga River. (So many cigars were made in the Conestoga water basin that a local cigar named the "Conestoga" became known as a "stogie" throughout the frontiers of the United States.)

Hunsecker's Mill Bridge

Hunsecker's Mill Bridge

Pinetown Bridge

GPS Coordinates: N 40 ° -6'-19.2" / W 76 ° -14'- 53.4"

History: The Pinetown Bridge was built in 1867 by the prolific bridge builder Elias McMellen. In 1972 the bridge was destroyed by Hurricane Agnes and in the following year the bridge was rebuilt by local Amish men. To prevent future damage from floods, the bridge foundation was raised 17.5 ft. above the water line.

Length: 124 feet
Width: 12 feet 10 inches

Pinetown Bridge

Pinetown Bridge

Landis Mill Bridge

GPS Coordinates: N 40 ° -4'-4.8" / W 76 ° -20'- 41.4"

History: The Landis Mill Bridge was built in 1873 by Elias McMellen. Since the bridge span is rather short, the construction uses king post trusses instead of the traditional Burr truss.

Length: 41 feet
Width: 13 feet

Landis Mill Bridge

Landis Mill Bridge

Kurtz Mill Bridge

GPS Coordinates: N 40 º -0'-48.6" / W 76 º -16'- 59.9"

History: The Kurtz Mill Bridge was built in 1876 by W.W. Upp over the Conestoga River. It was heavily damaged in 1972 by Hurricane Agnes and was repaired and moved to its present location in Lancaster County Park over the Mill Creek, which is a tributary of the Conestoga River.

Length: 94 feet
Width: 11 feet

Kurtz Mill Bridge

Kurtz Mill Bridge

Willow Hill Bridge

GPS Coordinates: N 40 ° -1'-39" / W 76 ° -12'- 11.9"

History: The Willow Hill Bridge, located just off Route 30 near the American Music Theater, was reconstructed in 1962 from parts of the Miller's Farm bridge, which was built in 1871 by Elias McMellen. The bridge is a single span with a double Burr arch truss.

Length: 93 feet
Width: 15 feet

Chickies Creek Tour

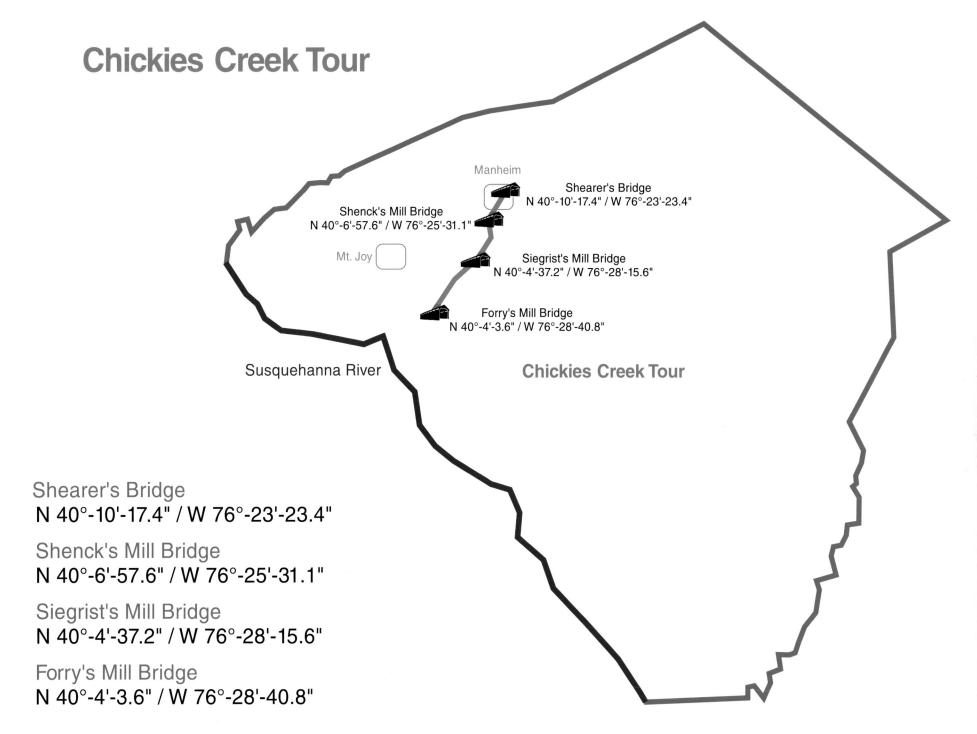

Manheim

Shearer's Bridge
N 40°-10'-17.4" / W 76°-23'-23.4"

Shenck's Mill Bridge
N 40°-6'-57.6" / W 76°-25'-31.1"

Mt. Joy

Siegrist's Mill Bridge
N 40°-4'-37.2" / W 76°-28'-15.6"

Forry's Mill Bridge
N 40°-4'-3.6" / W 76°-28'-40.8"

Susquehanna River

Chickies Creek Tour

Shearer's Bridge
N 40°-10'-17.4" / W 76°-23'-23.4"

Shenck's Mill Bridge
N 40°-6'-57.6" / W 76°-25'-31.1"

Siegrist's Mill Bridge
N 40°-4'-37.2" / W 76°-28'-15.6"

Forry's Mill Bridge
N 40°-4'-3.6" / W 76°-28'-40.8"

Shearer's Bridge

GPS Coordinates: N 40 ° -10'-17.4" / W 76 ° -23'- 23.4"

History: The Shearer's bridge spans the Big Chickies Creek and was built in 1847 by Jacob Clare. The bridge was moved in 1971 to its present location in the Manheim Memorial Park.

Length: 86 feet
Width: 15 feet

Shenck's Mill Bridge

GPS Coordinates: N 40 ° -6'-57.6" / W 76 ° -25'- 31.1"

History: The Shenck's Mill bridge, also know as Schenck's Mill bridge, was built in 1855 by Charles Malhorn and Levi Fink. The construction of this single span bridge is a double Burr truss with the addition of steel hanger rods.

Length: 80 feet
Width: 13 feet 10 inches

Shenck's Mill Bridge

Shenck's Mill Bridge

Siegrist's Mill Bridge

GPS Coordinates: N 40 ° -4'-37.2" / W 76 ° -28'- 15.6"

History: The Siegrist's Mill bridge was built in 1885 by James C. Carpenter. It was named by the Siegrist family, who lived nearby. It is painted inside and out using traditional red paint while the approaches are painted white.

Length: 92 feet
Width: 12 feet 9 inches

Siegrist's Mill Bridge

Siegrist's Mill Bridge

Forry's Mill Bridge

GPS Coordinates: N 40 ° -4'-3.6" / W 76 ° -28'- 40.8"

History: The Forry's Mill bridge was built in 1869 by Elias McMellen. The bridge is a single span, double Burr arch with the decking made of oak planks.

Length: 91 feet 6 inches
Width: 12 feet 10 inches

Forry's Mill Bridge

Forry's Mill Bridge

Pequea Creek Tour

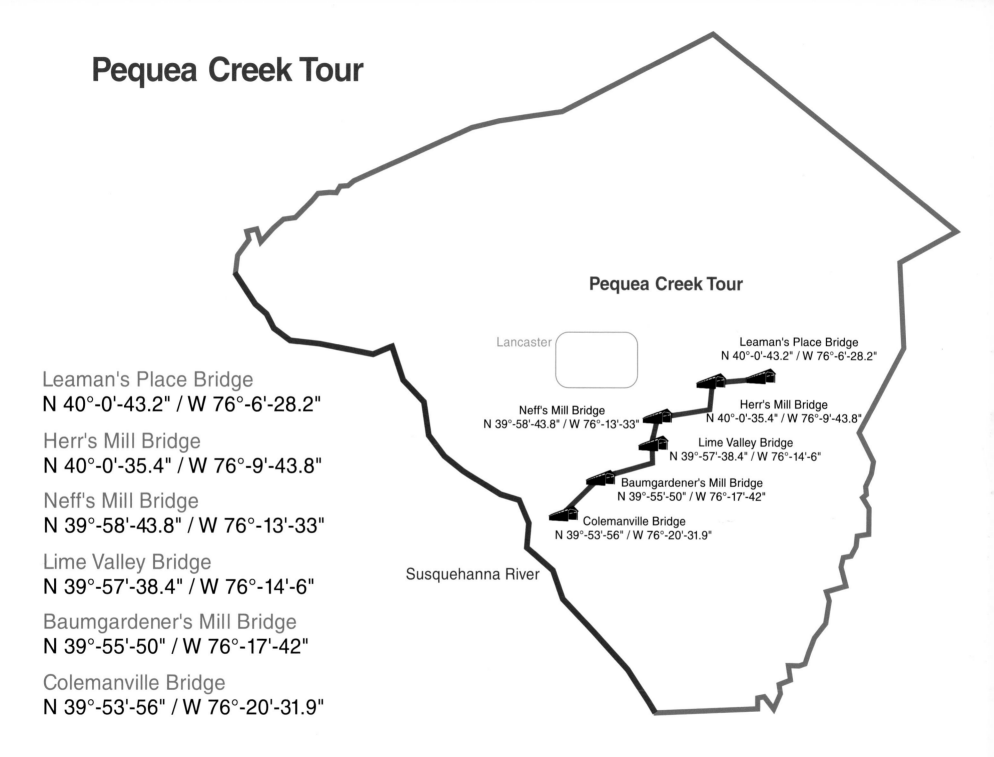

Leaman's Place Bridge
N 40°-0'-43.2" / W 76°-6'-28.2"

Herr's Mill Bridge
N 40°-0'-35.4" / W 76°-9'-43.8"

Neff's Mill Bridge
N 39°-58'-43.8" / W 76°-13'-33"

Lime Valley Bridge
N 39°-57'-38.4" / W 76°-14'-6"

Baumgardener's Mill Bridge
N 39°-55'-50" / W 76°-17'-42"

Colemanville Bridge
N 39°-53'-56" / W 76°-20'-31.9"

Pequea Creek Tour

Lancaster

Leaman's Place Bridge
N 40°-0'-43.2" / W 76°-6'-28.2"

Herr's Mill Bridge
N 40°-0'-35.4" / W 76°-9'-43.8"

Neff's Mill Bridge
N 39°-58'-43.8" / W 76°-13'-33"

Lime Valley Bridge
N 39°-57'-38.4" / W 76°-14'-6"

Baumgardener's Mill Bridge
N 39°-55'-50" / W 76°-17'-42"

Colemanville Bridge
N 39°-53'-56" / W 76°-20'-31.9"

Susquehanna River

Leaman's Place Bridge

GPS Coordinates: N 40 ° -0'-43.2" / W 76 ° -6'- 28.2"

History: The Leaman's Place bridge was built in 1845 by James C. Carpenter on land granted to the Mary Ferree family by William Penn. The bridge was rebuilt by Elias McMellen in 1893 and refurbished in 2004.

Length: 102 feet
Width: 15 feet

Leaman's Place Bridge

47

Leaman's Place Bridge

Herr's Mill Bridge

GPS Coordinates: N 40 ° -0'-35.4" / W 76 ° -9'- 43.8"

History: The Herr's Mill bridge was built in 1844 by Joseph Elliot and Robert Russell. It has a double span, double Burr arch truss construction. The bridge was later bypassed by a new concrete bridge and is currently on the private property of the Mill Village Camping Resort; however, you can view the bridge from the campground entrance road.

Length: 178 feet
Width: 15 feet

Neff's Mill Bridge

GPS Coordinates: N 39 º -58'-43.8" / W 76 º -13'- 33"

History: The Neff's Mill bridge was built in 1824 by Christian Breakbill. In 1875 it was rebuilt by James C. Carpenter. The single span bridge has the traditional double Burr arch truss and is probably the narrowest covered bridge in the county.

Length: 90 feet
Width: 11 feet 7 inches

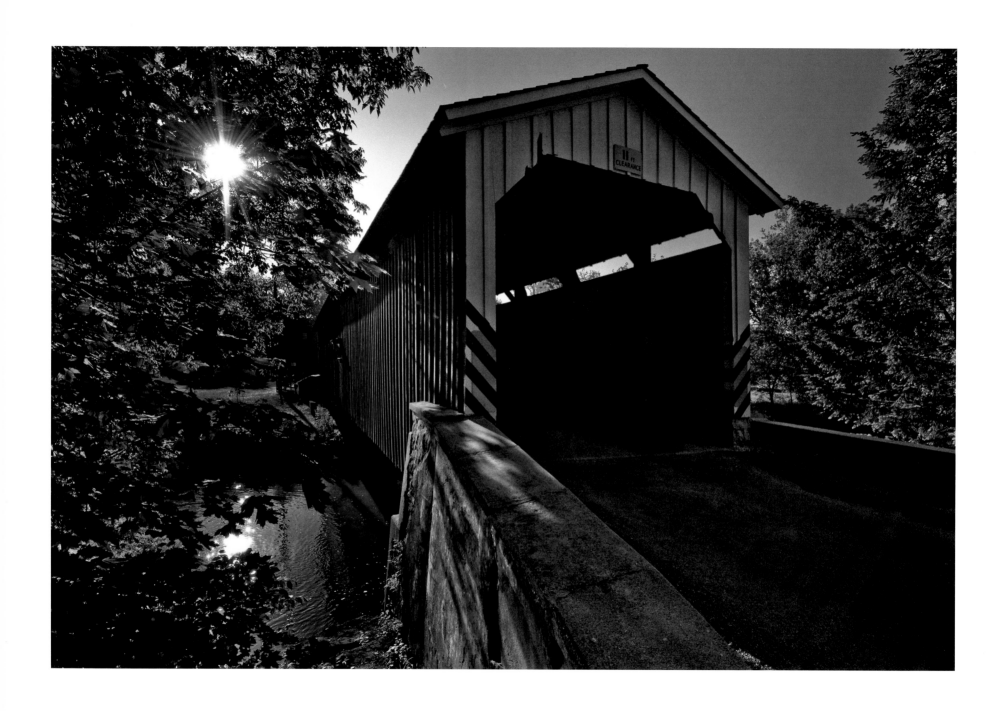

Neff's Mill Bridge

52

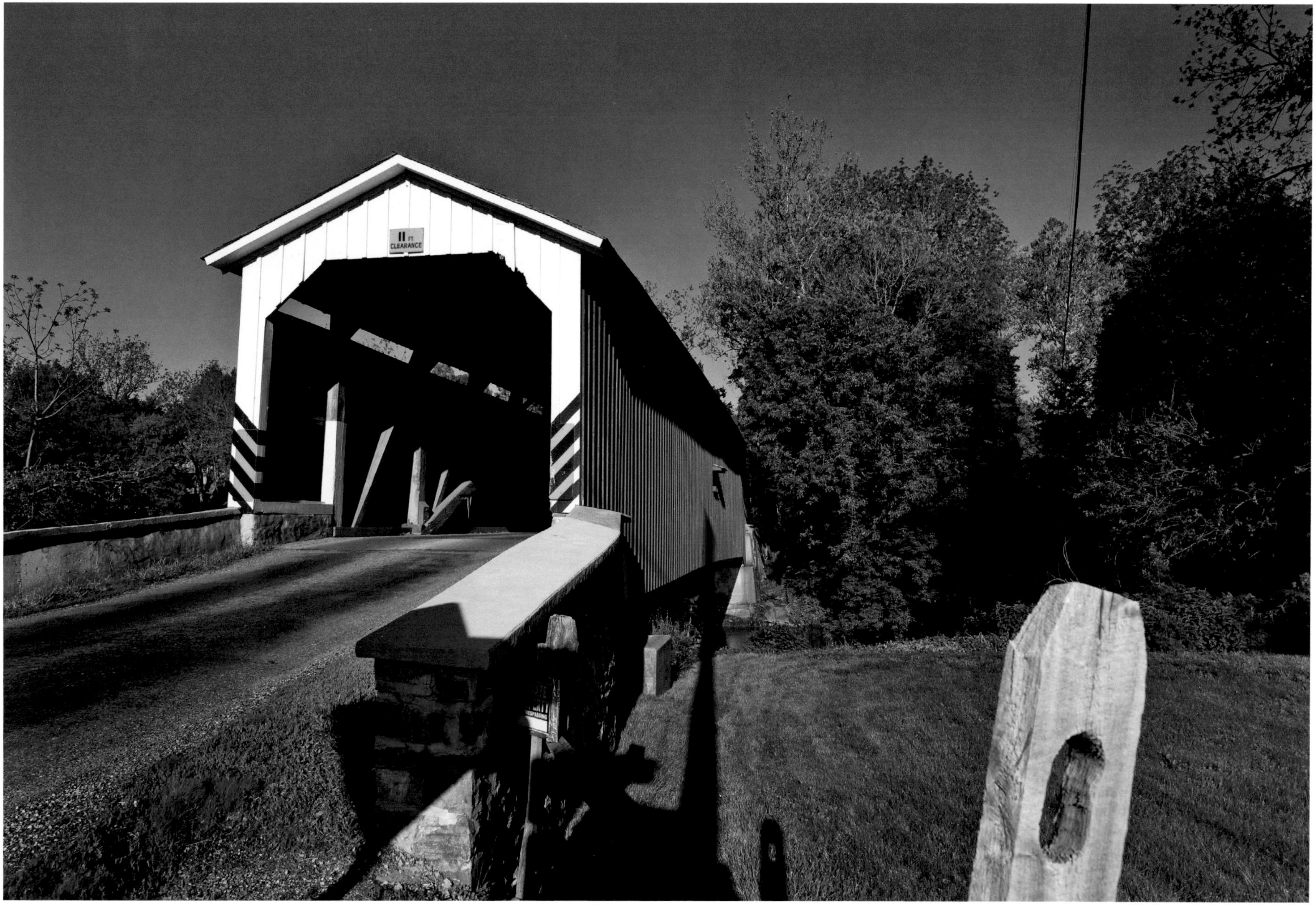

Neff's Mill Bridge

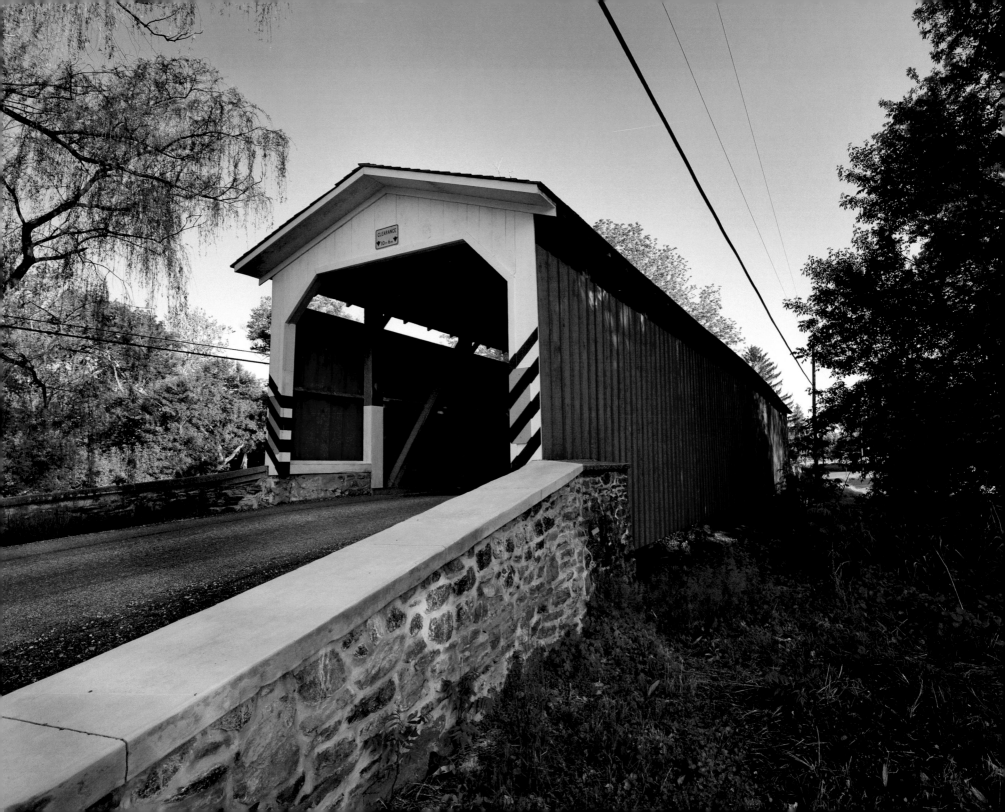

Lime Valley Bridge

GPS Coordinates: N 39 ° -57'-38.4" / W 76 ° -14'- 6"

History: The Lime Valley bridge was built in 1871 by Joseph Cramer. The bridge is a double Burr arch truss with the addition of steel hanger rods.

Length: 93 feet
Width: 13 feet

Baumgardener's Mill Bridge

GPS Coordinates: N 39 ° -55'-50" / W 76 ° -17'- 42"

History: The Baumgardener's Mill bridge was built in 1860 by Davis Kitch. In 1987 the bridge was restored and raised 4 feet to prevent any future flood damage.

Length: 120 feet
Width: 14 feet

Baumgardener's Mill Bridge

Baumgardener's Mill Bridge

Colemanville Bridge

GPS Coordinates: N 39 ° -53'-56" / W 76 ° -20'- 31.9"

History: The Colemanville bridge was built in 1856 by James C. Carpenter. After twice being damaged by floods, the bridge was rebuilt in 1938 and again in 1973 following Hurricane Agnes. In 1992, the bridge was completely restored and raised 6 feet on its foundation.

Length: 155 feet
Width: 14 feet

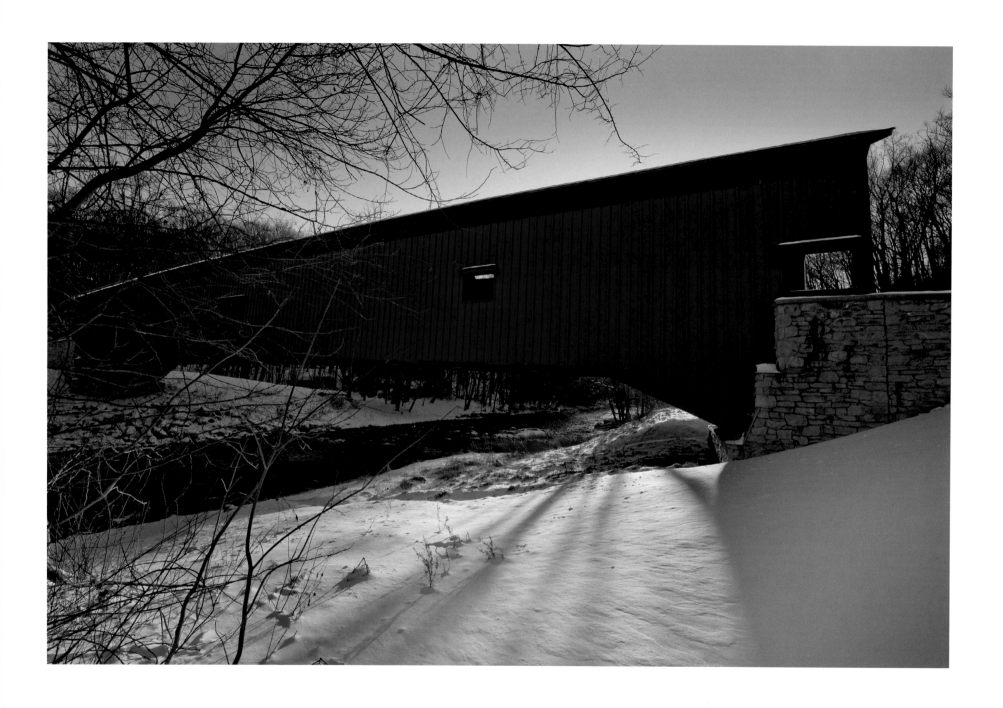

Colemanville Bridge

Colemanville Bridge

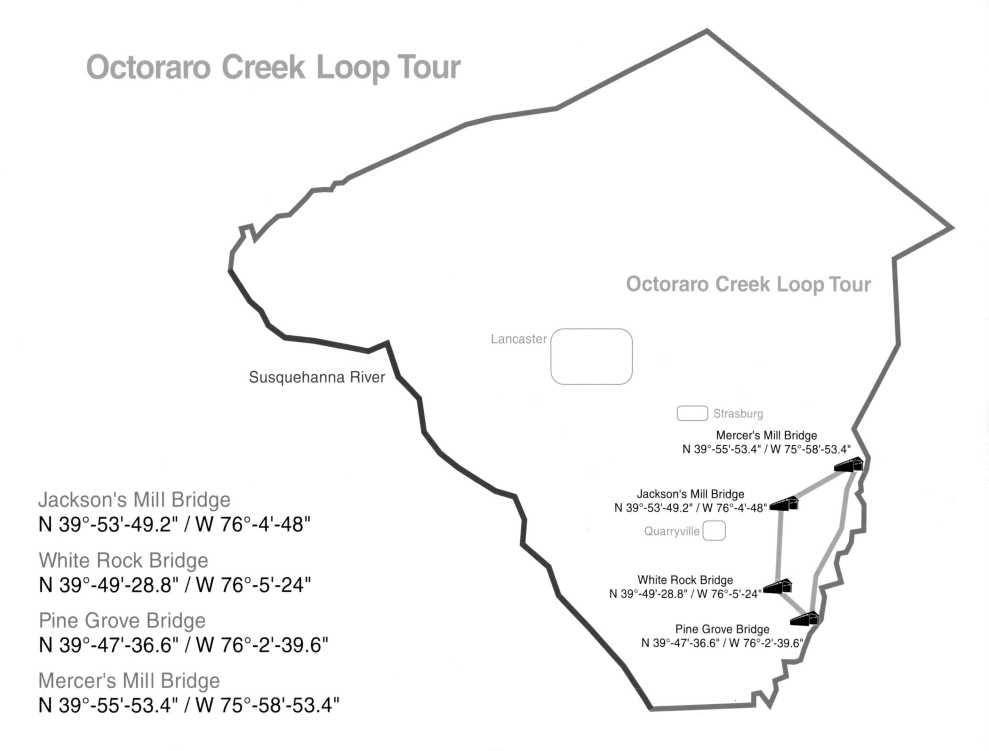

Octoraro Creek Loop Tour

Octoraro Creek Loop Tour

Lancaster

Susquehanna River

Strasburg

Mercer's Mill Bridge
N 39°-55'-53.4" / W 75°-58'-53.4"

Jackson's Mill Bridge
N 39°-53'-49.2" / W 76°-4'-48"

Quarryville

White Rock Bridge
N 39°-49'-28.8" / W 76°-5'-24"

Pine Grove Bridge
N 39°-47'-36.6" / W 76°-2'-39.6"

Jackson's Mill Bridge
N 39°-53'-49.2" / W 76°-4'-48"

White Rock Bridge
N 39°-49'-28.8" / W 76°-5'-24"

Pine Grove Bridge
N 39°-47'-36.6" / W 76°-2'-39.6"

Mercer's Mill Bridge
N 39°-55'-53.4" / W 75°-58'-53.4"

Jackson's Mill Bridge

GPS Coordinates: N 39 ° -53'-49.2" / W 76 ° -4'- 48"

History: The Jackson's Mill bridge was built in 1878 by John Smith and Samuel Stauffer. The bridge was rebuilt in 1985 and was again restored in 2005.

Length: 139 feet
Width: 14 feet

Jackson's Mill Bridge

Jackson's Mill Bridge

White Rock Bridge

GPS Coordinates: N 39 ° -49'-28.8" / W 76 ° -5'- 24"

History: The White Rock Forge bridge was built in 1847 by John Russell and rebuilt in 1884 by Elias McMellen.

Length: 103 feet
Width: 13 feet

White Rock Bridge

White Rock Bridge

Pine Grove Bridge

GPS Coordinates: N 39 ° -47'-36.6" / W 76 ° -2'- 39.6"

History: The Pine Grove bridge was built in 1884 by Elias McMellen. This bridge sits on the border between Lancaster and Chester counties. It is a double span, double Burr arch truss and is the longest covered bridge in Lancaster County. Both spans have been reenforced with steel beams to withstand the heavy traffic.

Length: 198 feet
Width: 15 feet

Pine Grove Bridge

Pine Grove Bridge

Pine Grove Bridge

Pine Grove Bridge

Mercer's Mill Bridge

GPS Coordinates: N 39 ° -55'-53.4" / W 75 ° -58'- 53.4"

History: The Mercer's Mill bridge was built in 1880 by B.J. Carter. Like the Pine Grove bridge, it borders Lancaster and Chester Counties. The bridge is a single span double Burr arch truss with an oak planked deck.

Length: 87 feet
Width: 15 feet 4 inches

Mercer's Mill Bridge

83

Mercer's Mill Bridge

Northeastern Lancaster County Loop Tour

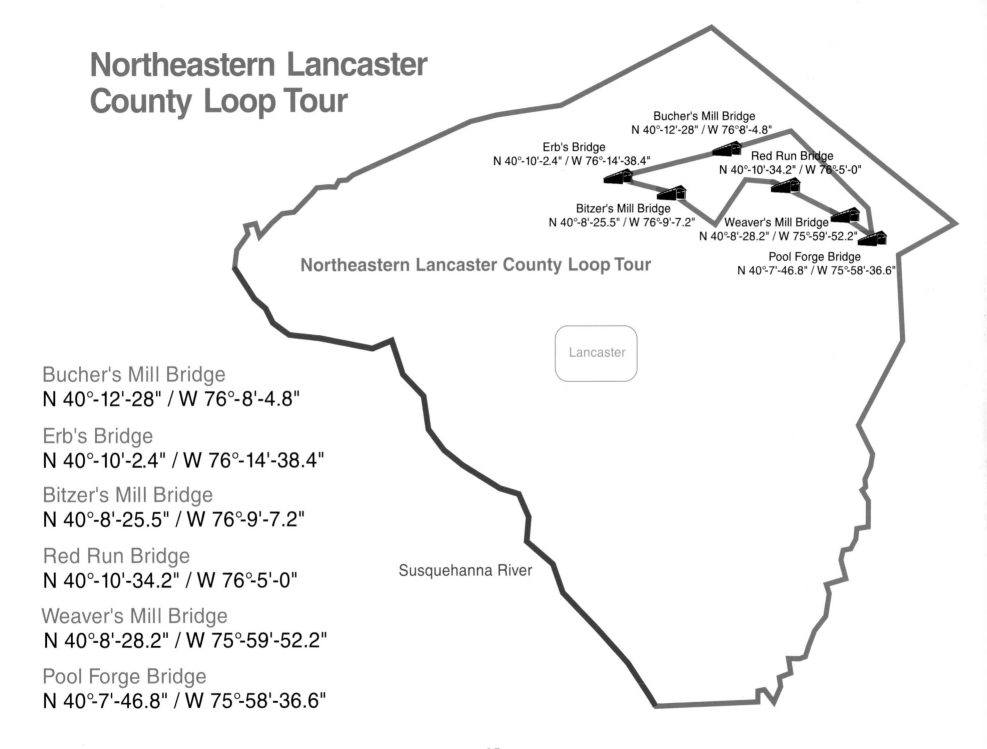

Bucher's Mill Bridge
N 40°-12'-28" / W 76°-8'-4.8"

Erb's Bridge
N 40°-10'-2.4" / W 76°-14'-38.4"

Red Run Bridge
N 40°-10'-34.2" / W 76°-5'-0"

Bitzer's Mill Bridge
N 40°-8'-25.5" / W 76°-9'-7.2"

Weaver's Mill Bridge
N 40°-8'-28.2" / W 75°-59'-52.2"

Pool Forge Bridge
N 40°-7'-46.8" / W 75°-58'-36.6"

Northeastern Lancaster County Loop Tour

Lancaster

Susquehanna River

Bucher's Mill Bridge
N 40°-12'-28" / W 76°-8'-4.8"

Erb's Bridge
N 40°-10'-2.4" / W 76°-14'-38.4"

Bitzer's Mill Bridge
N 40°-8'-25.5" / W 76°-9'-7.2"

Red Run Bridge
N 40°-10'-34.2" / W 76°-5'-0"

Weaver's Mill Bridge
N 40°-8'-28.2" / W 75°-59'-52.2"

Pool Forge Bridge
N 40°-7'-46.8" / W 75°-58'-36.6"

Bucher's Mill Bridge

GPS Coordinates: N 40 ° -12'-28" / W 76 ° -8'- 4.8"

History: The Bucher's Mill bridge was built in 1891 by Elias McMellen using a single span double Burr arch construction. The following year the bridge was heavily damaged by flooding and was rebuilt by Elias McMellen.

Length: 54 feet
Width: 13 feet 3 inches

Bucher's Mill Bridge

Bucher's Mill Bridge

Erb's Bridge

GPS Coordinates: N 40 ° -10'-2.4" / W 76 ° -14'- 38.4"

History: The Erb's bridge was built in 1849 for a cost of $1,700. The bridge spans the Hammer Creek and in 1887 was rebuilt by John G. Bowman.

Length: 70 feet
Width: 13 feet 1 inches

Erb's Bridge

Erb's Bridge

Bitzer's Mill Bridge

GPS Coordinates: N 40 º -8'-25.5" / W 76 º -9'- 7"

History: The Bitzer's Mill bridge was built in 1846 by George Fink and Sam Reamsnyder. Later steel beams were added to the span to support the oldest covered bridge in Lancaster County.

Length: 98 feet
Width: 13 feet 1 inches

Bitzer's Mill Bridge

Bitzer's Mill Bridge

Red Run Bridge

GPS Coordinates: N 40 ° -10'-34.2" / W 76 ° -5'- 0"

History: The Red Run bridge was built in 1866 by Elias McMellen and once spanned the Muddy Creek but now is situated next to the Red Run Campground.

Length: 107 feet
Width: 15 feet

Red Run Bridge

Red Run Bridge

Weaver's Mill Bridge

GPS Coordinates: N 40 ° -8'-28.2" / W 75 ° -59'- 52.2"

History: The Weaver's Mill bridge was built in 1878 by B. C. Carter and
J. F. Stauffer and spans the Conestoga River. The bridge has a single span
with a double Burr arch truss.

Length: 85 feet
Width: 15 feet

Weaver's Mill Bridge

Weaver's Mill Bridge

Pool Forge Bridge

GPS Coordinates: N 40 ° -7'-46.8" / W 75 ° -58'- 36.6"

History: The Pool Forge bridge was built in 1859 by Levi Frank and Elias McMellen. The bridge spans the Conestoga River and is located on private property, but it is easily viewed from a parking area adjacent to the main road.

Length: 99 feet
Width: 15 feet

Pool Forge Bridge

Pool Forge Bridge

Pool Forge Bridge

Pool Forge Bridge